For Di and Logan, and for anyone who's ever daydreamed
of having a giant robot to smash up their school.

For lots more awesome *Mo-bot High* stuff, go to:

www.mobot-high.com

MO-BOT HIGH
A DAVID FICKLING BOOK 978 1 849 92171 8

This part 1 of book 1 first published in hardback with part 2 in 2010,
thanks to the amazing DFC weekly comic.

Published in Great Britain in 2010 by David Fickling Books,
a division of Random House Children's Publishers UK
A Random House Group Company
This edition published 2013

1 3 5 7 9 10 8 6 4 2

Copyright © Neill Cameron, 2010

The right of Neill Cameron to be identified as the author of this work has been
asserted in accordance with the Copyright, Designs and Patents Act 1988.

All rights reserved. No part of this publication may be reproduced, stored in a retrieval system,
or transmitted in any form or by any means, electronic, mechanical, photocopying,
recording or otherwise, without the prior permission of the publishers.

DAVID FICKLING BOOKS, 31 Beaumont Street, Oxford, OX1 2NP

www.**randomhousechildrens**.co.uk
www.**randomhouse**.co.uk

Addresses for companies within The Random House Group Limited can be found at:
www.randomhouse.co.uk/offices.htm
THE RANDOM HOUSE GROUP Limited Reg. No. 954009
A CIP catalogue record for this book is available from the British Library.
Printed in China

The Random House Group Limited supports the Forest Stewardship Council® (FSC®), the leading international
forest-certification organisation. Our books carrying the FSC label are printed on FSC®-certified paper. FSC is the
only forest-certification scheme supported by the leading environmental organisations, including Greenpeace.
Our paper procurement policy can be found at www.randomhouse.co.uk/environment

MO-BOT HIGH

BOOK ONE

by NEILL CAMERON

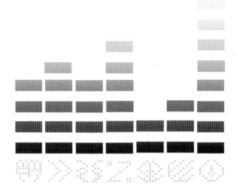

PART ONE

GET READY FOR *MO-BOTS!*

FOR *DIGITAL ROBOTIC COMBATSUITS* IN *THRILLING, TITANIC BATTLES!*

GET READY FOR *EXCITEMENT* ON A *WHOLE NEW LEVEL!*

BUT FIRST... GET READY FOR *DOUBLE GEOGRAPHY.*

THIS IS IT, THEN...

I'M DOOMED.

DON'T BE SILLY, SWEETIE.

IT'S NOT THE END OF THE WORLD, JUST A NEW SCHOOL.

YEAH. LIKE I SAY --

DOOMED.

ASHA

YOU'RE NOT GOING CRAZY.

I MEAN, AS FAR AS I KNOW.

THEY'RE *REAL?!*

WHAT... WHAT *ARE* THEY?

MO-BOTS.

MO-WHATS?

BOTS.

YOU KNOW... DMCS.

'DEE EM CEES'?

I DON'T...

WHAT DOES THAT MEAN?

DIGITAL MOBILE COMBAT-SUITS.

SORRY, HANG ON... *WHAT???*

HI! ARE YOU NEW? MY NAME'S SHELLY. I LOVE YOUR BAG!

IS THAT VAMPANDA? SO CUTE! WHERE DID YOU GET IT?

...HUH?

UM, SORRY, I MEAN - AT CAMDEN MARKET?

OH, ARE YOU FROM LONDON, THEN?

THAT MUST BE SO GREAT!

WELL, I...

IT MUST BE SO EXCITING! NOT LIKE BORING OLD MIDDLEFORD.

HONESTLY, IT'S RUBBISH ROUND HERE, NOTHING EVER HAPPENS.

WHAT DID YOU SAY YOUR NAME WAS AGAIN?

ASHA! UM... BUT, WHAT ABOUT THOSE...?

SO, HOW COME YOU GOT BANISHED TO THIS DUMP OF A TOWN, ANYWAY?

WHO'S CALLING IT A DUMP OF A TOWN??

SHE DID!

THE NEW GIRL!

WHERE ARE YOU FROM, THEN?

LONDON, SHE SAID.

OOOH, LONDON!

WHAT, YOU THINK YOU'RE TOO GOOD FOR US, 'LONDON'?

NO, I...

SHE DOES! SHE THINKS SHE'S TOO GOOD FOR US!

...CHALLENGE?

CHALLENGE!

BPPPP BPPPP!!

IT'S A CHALLENGE! YOU'D BETTER ANSWER IT!

...WHAT?

NO, SERIOUSLY, YOU BETTER HAD.

YOU'RE ALL CRAZY! YOU'RE A BUNCH OF CRAZY PEOPLE!

LOOK, JUST PRESS 'ACCEPT'...

...THERE YOU GO!

WHAT...? WHERE...?

GOOD MORNING, ASHA.

...

...NO WAY!

GO ON, GEMMA!

ZAP HER SILLY!

HA! THIS IS GOING TO BE EASY!

HEY, HANG ON! TIME OUT, TIME OUT!

I DON'T THINK SO!

KRRZZOWWW!!!!

OW! HEY!!

COME ON, ROBOT THINGY, HIT HER BACK!

UNKNOWN COMMAND - 313 ERROR

AARGH! STUPID!!

DID YOU JUST CALL ME STUPID?

NO, I--

OH, THAT IS IT!

KRRZZAAAKK!!

TEACHER? UH-OH...

MINIMISE!

WHAT?

QUICKLY! A TEACHER'S COMING!

HURRY UP AND EXIT!!

AARGH! HOW DO I DO THAT?!

MENU BUTTON! THE BIG ONE IN THE MIDDLE!

UM... OH, OKAY...

COME ON, ROBOT THINGY..!

WHOA!

WHAT ARE YOU ALL DOING STANDING AROUND?

NOTHING, MISS!

WELL, GET OFF TO CLASSES! THE BELL WENT FIVE MINUTES AGO!

YES, MISS.

WE'RE NOT DONE, LONDON.

WOW. WHAT'S HER *PROBLEM?*

I MEAN, WHAT DID I EVER DO TO *HER?*

DON'T WORRY ABOUT HER. YOU DID GOOD!

YEAH, FOR YOUR FIRST GO THAT WAS ACTUALLY PRETTY IMPRESSIVE.

IT WAS?

HI, I'M JESSICA.

I'M SOPHIE.

UM... I'M ASHA. HI!

WELCOME TO THE SCHOOL, ASHA!

WE'LL BE KEEPING AN EYE ON HOW YOU GET ON...

OH, OKAY.

WHAT?

COME ON, LET'S GET OFF TO LESSONS! OOH, I HOPE THEY PUT YOU IN MY CLASS.

WE CAN SIT TOGETHER AND I'LL SHOW YOU ROUND AND TELL YOU *ALL* THE GOSS AND WE CAN BE *BEST FRIENDS!*

UM... YAY?

TUESDAY. LUNCHTIME.

SO - SECOND DAY ALREADY! ARE YOU HAVING FUN YET?

FUN? *FUN?* THIS WHOLE SCHOOL IS COMPLETELY INSANE!

HOW DO YOU MEAN?

ARE YOU *KIDDING?* SHELLY, EVERYONE HAS GIANT *ROBOTS* THAT ZAP OUT OF THEIR *PHONES!*

...AND?

I MEAN... YOU DO KNOW THAT'S NOT NORMAL, RIGHT?

IT'S NORMAL *HERE.*

YOU'RE JUST NEW, YOU'LL GET USED TO IT!

BUT... DON'T YOU THINK IT'S *WEIRD?* I MEAN, THESE 'DMCS' - WHERE DO THEY COME FROM, ANYWAY?

OH, *I* DUNNO. THEY'VE BEEN AROUND PRETTY MUCH FOREVER.

FOREVER?

WELL, ALICE BARTON'S SISTER NINA'S IN YEAR 12, AND THEY WERE AROUND WHEN *SHE* STARTED, SO... YEAH! FOR*EVER*-EVER!

...SO FIRST, THERE'S DMC RACES: *SPEED BATTLES!*

NOW, NEELA CRUDUP WAS LAST YEAR'S SPEED-CHAMPION, BUT HER PARENTS MOVED TO SCOTLAND, SO *ANYONE* COULD WIN THIS YEAR.

ACTUALLY, KEEP IT TO YOURSELF, BUT I RECKON IT COULD BE ME THIS TIME.

IF I...

WHAT ARE THOSE GUYS DOING?

WHO, THEM? I DUNNO, *NERD* STUFF.

I THINK THEY CALL IT 'CODING-BATTLES' OR SOMETHING.

ANYWAY, WHO CARES? I THOUGHT YOU WANTED TO MEET THE *COOL* PEOPLE?

SO WHERE ARE ALL THE BOYS? DON'T THEY *HAVE* MO-BOTS?

THEY *DO*, BUT ALL THEY DO IS PLAY MECHA-FOOTBALL ALL DAY LONG. IT'S *TOTALLY* BORING.

ANYWAY, THIS IS MORE LIKE IT. OVER THERE – THAT'S JESSICA PARKER AND SOPHIE ONGANDZI.

I THINK I MET THEM ALREADY. WHO ARE THEY?

WHO ARE *THEY???*

JESSICA PARKER!! WOW, WHERE TO START? SHE'S CAPTAIN OF THE MECHAHOCKEY TEAM! SHE WAS LAST YEAR'S OVERALL DMC-CHAMPION! SHE'S *NEVER LOST* A FASHION BATTLE!

'FASHION BATTLE'?

YOU'LL SEE.

THAT GIRL WITH HER, THAT'S SOPHIE ONGANDZI – THEY'RE LIKE *BEST FRIENDS*, AND THEY PILOT TOGETHER IN TAG BATTLES. SOPHIE'S THE SCHOOL'S REIGNING *DMC DANCE BATTLE* CHAMP!

AND SHE'S GOT *SUCH GREAT HAIR!*

JESSSICA

SOPHIE

SO YEAH, THOSE TWO... WELL, THEY'RE PRETTY MUCH THE *COOLEST.*

AND WHAT'S MORE, THEY'RE ACTUALLY REALLY NICE!

ANYWAY, COME ON! WE'VE ONLY GOT A FEW MINUTES LEFT FOR LUNCH, AND I WANT TO GET A PRACTICE RACE IN!

YEAH... COMING...

OOOF!!

HEY!!

MY CHIPS!!

OH, I'M SO SORRY!

OH LOOK, IT'S LONDON.

YOU ARE SO FOR IT NOW.

'OOOH, I'M FROM LONDON SO I'M TOO GOOD TO LOOK WHERE I'M GOING...'

HEY, I SAID I WAS SORRY, OKAY?

ARE YOU GONNA LET HER GET AWAY WITH THAT, GEMMA?

...HEY, CALM DOWN.

I WAS REALLY LOOKING FORWARD TO THOSE!

OOH, CHALLENGE!

CHALLENGE!

BRRRNNNNGGG!

AW, CHEAT!

SAVED BY THE BELL!

I GUESS WE'D BETTER BE GETTING OFF TO CLASSES, HUH?

DON'T THINK YOU'RE GETTING OFF THAT EASY.

THIS FRIDAY. AFTER SCHOOL. WASTE GROUND, BEHIND THE SCIENCE BLOCK. NO BELL TO SAVE YOU, NO TEACHERS.

WE'RE GOING TO FINISH THIS. AND I'M GOING TO FINISH YOU.

WEDNESDAY. 6:41 PM, ASHA'S HOUSE.

TIME UNTIL FIGHT: 43 HRS 49 MINS...

OH, COME ON!

I NEED TO *PRACTISE!* WHY WON'T YOU *WORK?!*

HUH?

DMCapp
DMC System unavailable

Unauthorised Location

'UNAUTHORISED LOCATION'? WHAT'S *THAT* MEAN?

DOES IT ONLY WORK AT THE SCHOOL?

AAA-SHA! DINNER'S READY!

COMING, DAD!

OH COME *ON* - DON'T YOU 'CONNECTION ERROR' ME...

AARGH! I GIVE UP!!

ASHA!!

I'M COMING...

BRRP

DMCapp
DMC messaging

INCOMING MESSAGE

BRRP

DMCapp
DMC messaging

INCOMING MESSAGE

BRRP

DMCapp
DMC messaging

1 missed message
DMCid: <unknown>

THURSDAY. 8:21 AM.

TIME UNTIL FIGHT: 32 HRS 09 MINS...

SERIOUSLY, I'M PRETTY SURE I'M SICK.

YOU DON'T LOOK SICK.

I'M COMING DOWN WITH SOMETHING! I SHOULD REALLY PROBABLY JUST GO HOME TO BED.

ASHA... IS THERE ANYTHING WRONG? YOU'VE BEEN IN A FUNNY MOOD ALL WEEK.

IT'S FINE, I'M JUST ILL IS ALL.

LOOK, IF YOU'RE REALLY NOT FEELING BETTER BY TONIGHT, YOU CAN CURL UP ON THE SOFA AND I'LL COOK SOMETHING NICE. BUTTERNUT SQUASH SOUP!

YEAH, OKAY...

...

...YOU KNOW, YOU DON'T HAVE TO WALK ME TO SCHOOL EVERY DAY...

HA HA HA HA HA!

KISSY KISSY BUTTERNUT SQUASH!

DON'T BE SILLY, IT'S ON MY WAY.

OKAY, YOU HAVE A GOOD DAY, DARLING!

LOVE YOU!

YEAH.

...THANKS, DAD.

HA HA HA!

HAVE A GOOD DAY, DAAAHLING!

HA HA HA HA HA!

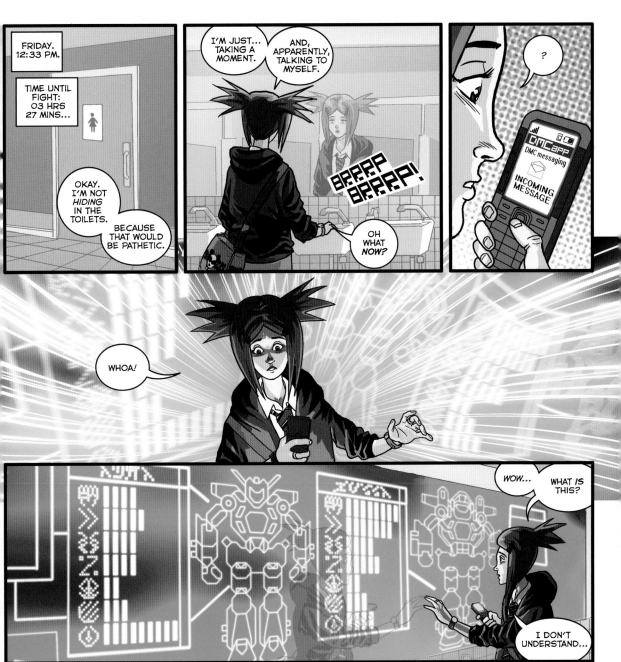

FRIDAY. 12:33 PM.

TIME UNTIL FIGHT: 03 HRS 27 MINS...

OKAY. I'M NOT *HIDING* IN THE TOILETS.

BECAUSE THAT WOULD BE PATHETIC.

I'M JUST... TAKING A MOMENT.

AND, APPARENTLY, TALKING TO MYSELF.

BR.R.R.P! BR.R.R.P!

OH WHAT *NOW?*

?

DMC messaging

INCOMING MESSAGE

WHOA!

WOW... WHAT *IS* THIS?

I DON'T UNDERSTAND...

ARE YOU TRYING TO *TELL* ME SOMETHING?

THAT SIGN - WHAT *IS* THAT?

WHO'S *DOING* THIS?

SLAM!

HEY! WHAT?

WAIT!

...UM.

HEY, YOU SHOWED UP. GOOD FOR YOU!

GOOD LUCK!

OH... THANKS.

...YOU'RE GOING TO *NEED* IT.

ALRIGHT, LONDON? YOU READY TO BATTLE?

BRRRP! BRRRP!

LOOK... CAN'T WE JUST *TALK* ABOUT THIS?

OH, *BLAH BLAH BLAH!* JUST *FIGHT*, WILL YOU?!

DMCapp

INCOMING CHALLENGE

DMCid: Gemma_B

...

YOU KNOW WHAT?

FINE.

ACTIVATE!

KKKPPPZZOWWW!!!

...THIS IS GOING TO BE *AWESOME!*

GOOD AFTERNOON, ASHA.

GOOD AFTERNOON, ROBOT THINGY. I DON'T SUPPOSE YOU'RE GOING TO BE ANY MORE HELPFUL THIS TIME?

UNKNOWN COMMAND - 313 ERROR.

THOUGHT NOT.

LOOK AT HER, STILL USING THAT PUNY BASIC MODEL DMC.

THIS IS GOING TO BE A PUSHOVER!

USE IT AS A CHANCE TO PRACTISE.

SHOW OFF, TRY SOME SPECIAL MOVES - SEE IF YOU CAN BEAT YOUR OWN BEST SCORE.

SERIOUSLY. LET'S *ANNIHILATE* THIS GIRL.

YOU GOT IT.

COME ON THEN, ROBOT THINGY. LET'S GO GET DEMOLISHED.

UNKNOWN COMMAND - 313 ERROR.

WONDERFUL.

CHALLENGE ON!

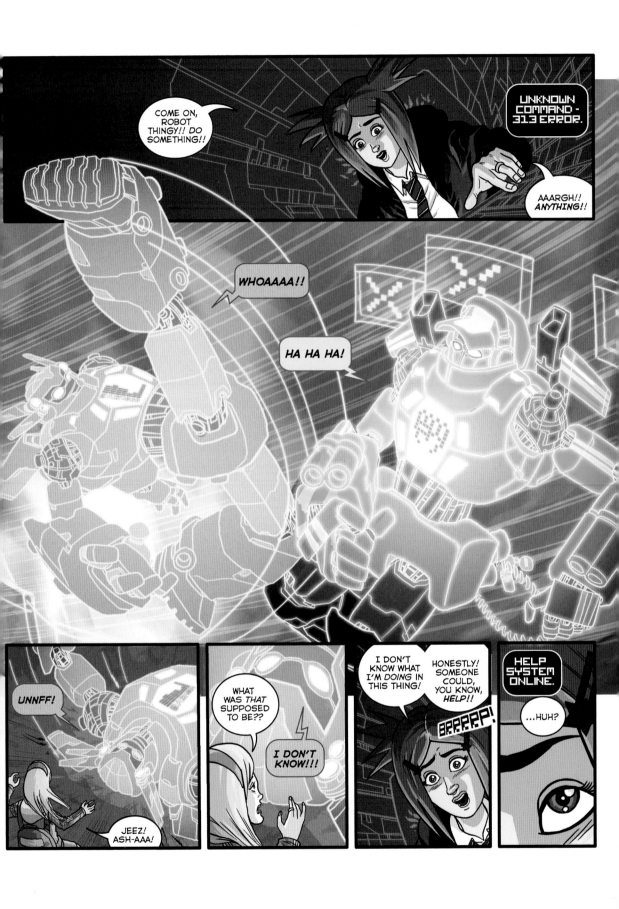

BZZZZZTTW!!!
KZZZZTMM!!!

OW OW OW OW OW!! HOW IS THAT NOT CHEATING?

THAT SIGN THINGY... I'VE SEEN THAT!

IN THE MIRROR THAT TIME!

SELECT OPERATION MODE.

I'M TRYING!

THERE!

WWMMMMMM...

?

SPIRIT MODE: ACTIVATE!

KEEP ON HER!

OH, DON'T WORRY.

LIGHTNING DASH HOCKEY STICK ATTACK!!!

OOOFF!

THERE GOES THE SCIENCE BLOCK.

AGAIN.

YEAH!

...NNGH...

GO ON!!

FINISH IT!!!

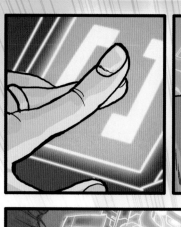

...HUH?

OOOH!

BLOCKED!

THERE YOU GO!

HEY, YOU KNOW WHAT?

I THINK I'M GETTING THE HANG OF THIS.

THIS IS IT, RIGHT?

YOU JUST PRESS THE *GLOWING* ONES, IN THE RIGHT ORDER...

...LIKE SO!

BKKZOOWWWWW!!!

WOW - ASHA'S CHARGING UP!

HER FOCUS RATING - IT'S SPIKING OFF THE CHARTS!

WHAT?

WHO ASKED YOU?!

HERE'S AN IDEA, GEMMA:

YOU DON'T PICK ON PEOPLE!

HOW ABOUT THAT??

YOU DON'T ACT RUDE AND MEAN FOR NO REASON!

AND YOU DON'T - EVER - MENTION MY MUM!

KRRRZAMMMM!!!!!

NO... WAY...

KRRRZOOWWWWM!!!!

OH WOW, YOU GOT *100 POINTS!* THAT'S INCREDIBLE!

POINTS?

'POINTS'? WHAT DO I WANT WITH POINTS?

THEY'RE *POINTS!* YOU CAN, YOU KNOW, CUSTOMISE YOUR DMC AND STUFF! GET AN UPGRADE!

YOU'RE KIDDING. WHAT IS THIS, GIANT ROBOT LOYALTY CARDS?

JUST SAVE THEM*!!*

OKAY, OKAY...

HI - ASHA? WELL DONE!

THAT WAS REALLY PRETTY AWESOME.

SERIOUSLY, GOOD FOR YOU. THAT GEMMA BOWLES HAS HAD IT COMING FOR AGES.

OH, UM ... HAS SHE?

OH, ABSOLUTELY. JUST A SHAME YOU COULDN'T TAKE OUT *SASHA* WHILE YOU WERE AT IT.

MAYBE *NEXT* TIME!

WHAT?

LISTEN, IF YOU LIKE, MAYBE WE COULD HANG OUT MONDAY - AT LUNCH?

WE COULD SHOW YOU HOW TO DO YOUR UPGRADES AND STUFF.

OOH, WE CAN TOTALLY *MAKEOVER* YOUR DMC!

MONDAY? UM, YEAH! THAT WOULD BE GREAT!

SEE YOU THEN, THEN!

HAVE A GOOD WEEKEND!

BYE-EEE!!

OH, THIS IS GOING TO BE SO COOL!

YEAH?

SO COOL! ASHA, IF YOU CAN PILOT LIKE THAT WE ARE GOING PLACES! YOU COULD MAKE THE TOP TEN! YOU COULD EVEN BE PILOT CHAMPION!!

'CHAMPION'?

...WELL I GUESS THAT WOULD BE OKAY.

SORRY, SASHA. I THOUGHT I HAD HER.

YEAH, WELL. GUESS NOT.

I DON'T GET IT. HOW DID SHE DO THAT?

DON'T WORRY ABOUT IT.

WE'LL GET HER LATER.

ASHA

FULL NAME: Asha Fakhri McGregor
AGE: 12
FRIENDS: Shelly. Hopefully more soon?
ENEMIES: Sasha and her gang seem to have taken a dislike.
FAVOURITE FOOD: Vegetable Okonomiyaki.
BONUS FACTS:
Asha has moved house 13 times in the last 7 years.
Asha is VAMPANDA's Number 1 Fan!

Shelly

SOPHIE

Jessica

FULL NAME: Shelly Milner
AGE: 12
FRIENDS: Has latched onto Asha. Seems to know *everybody*.
ENEMIES: Now who could dislike Shelly?
FAVOURITE FOOD: Pop Tarts
BONUS FACTS:
Shelly can sing all the words to every single number in *Prep School Singalong*.
Shelly secretly quite likes books about elves and fairies and such.

FULL NAME: Sophie Ongandzi
AGE: 12
FRIENDS: Best friends with Jessica.
ENEMIES: You'd know about it pretty quick.
FAVOURITE FOOD: Rice pudding with marmalade.
BONUS FACTS:
Sophie played the role of Macbeth in last year's school play.
Sophie can make her Mo-bot spin on its head for over two minutes.

FULL NAME: Jessica Janine Parker
AGE: 12
FRIENDS: Best friends with Sophie. Everyone else *wishes*.
ENEMIES: Above such petty concerns as 'having enemies'.
FAVOURITE FOOD: Sushi
BONUS FACTS:
Jessica knows more about fashion than most magazine editors.
Jessica is ALWAYS On Trend.

SASHA

FULL NAME: Sasha Marillion Goody
AGE: 12
FRIENDS: Gemma, Shaneele. Although 'lackeys' would be more appropriate.
ENEMIES: The world in general. Asha in particular.
FAVOURITE FOOD: Beef & Onion Pot Noodle
BONUS FACTS:
Sasha totally fancies Nick Parfitt in Year 10.
Sasha will BEAT YOU UP.

SHANEELE

GEMMA

FULL NAME: Shaneele Parfitt
AGE: 12
FRIENDS: Sasha, Gemma
ENEMIES: Anyone Sasha tells her
FAVOURITE FOOD: Marshmallow sandwiches
BONUS FACTS:
Shaneele once ate a jar of instant coffee granules for a bet.
Shaneele has never lost a game of ping-pong. EVER.

FULL NAME: Gemma Margaret Bowles
AGE: 12
FRIENDS: Sasha, Shaneele
ENEMIES: Asha, apparently
FAVOURITE FOOD: Chips
BONUS FACTS:
Gemma has a dog named 'Andre'.
Gemma can burp the theme tune to 'Animal Hospital'.

DMC
User Guide

Before using your new Digital Mobile Combatsuit (DMC), please take a moment to familiarise yourself with its components.

A: CENTRAL DISPLAY PANEL
B: ALERT PANELS
C: USC CUSTOMISATION PORTS
D: SECONDARY OPTICAL SYSTEM
[2 GIGAPIXEL]
E: PRIMARY OPTICAL SYSTEM
[8 GIGALPIXEL]

F: OMNINET TRANSCEIVERS
G: PILOT
H: STABILISERS
I: ONLINE PREDICTIVE TACTICAL INTERFACE SYSTEM

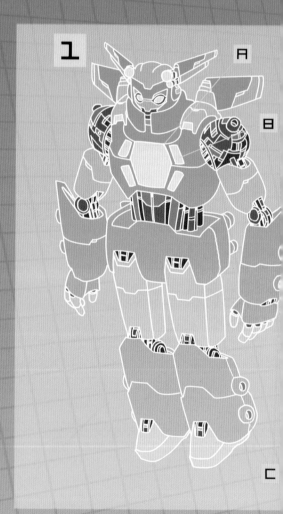

Default Model DMC
DMCid: <Asha>

1: EXO-ARMOUR VIEW
2: EXPLODED VIEW
3: INTERNAL SYSTEM VIEW

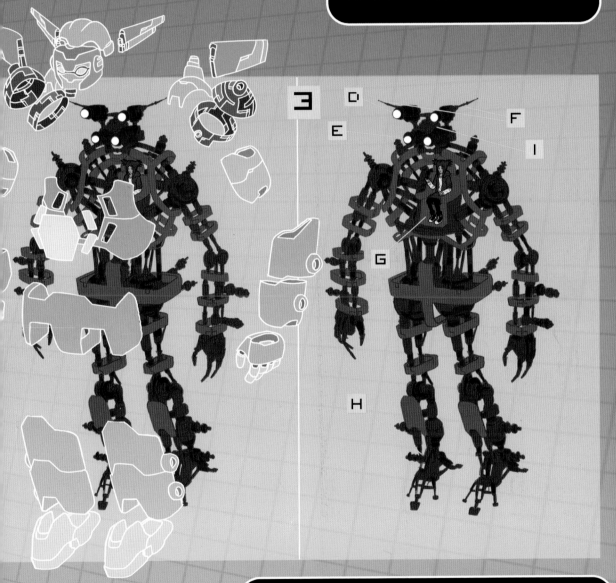

THE DFC LIBRARY:

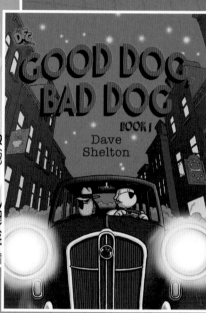

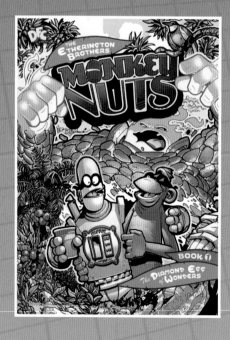